AF426582

Radiant Poppy

ALSO BY KELLY LYNN CURRY:

Breath and Bone
In This Flesh

RADIANT POPPY

BY

Kelly Lynn Curry

With poems illustrated by
Laura A. Clift

Dedicated to Matt.

For all that you've done.
The small and the monumental. For every second that you have held my hand through the agony. It was more than I could handle alone, and you made sure that I knew I was not. For doing whatever it took to help me through it all and never complaining. Reminding me I have made it this far and the pain has not killed me yet.
Thank you for being my forever hype man.

Hope: radiating through the haze

As the poppy grows

The pain disintegrates in my veins

As relief mounts ever still

The poppies bid the ache to flee

Coaxing pain to dissipate

Until my body is anesthetized

While Hope roars through my bones

Note from the Author

Writing about HOPE is harder than I thought it would be. Something so omnipresent yet intangible. It eludes me. Hope is so pertinent, but how does one define it?

I have lived with hope present in my life for the past four years. Sometimes, it was hard to grasp. Sometimes, it felt as if it was mocking me and I just wanted to give up, yet hope was always there. Forever embedded in me to never surrender; to never submit to the darkness. Ingrained in my fingertips. Deep-rooted in my footsteps.
Every part of me breathed HOPE.

Staying in the Cardiac ward, having fluid drained out of my body, was such an eye-opening experience. So much so that I wove hope tightly around my body, absorbing every ounce of it into my soul. I was determined to fight through the pain. This cataclysmic feeling pushed me forward through it all. It propelled me forward to the person I am today.

Kelly Lynn Curry

I have spent countless hours living in the Emergency Room and Hospital. This collection is about both the physical and emotional, that I was forced to face. From the intense feelings of morphine entering my bloodstream to trying to find Hope when I felt lost in the chaos of it all.

I tried to find something good in all the negativity surrounding me: lost friends, disability, and pain, so much pain. There is always something good that can be found in it all. I found Hope, Love, and Friendships. The independence, the strength, and the knowledge. I wouldn't trade the pain for what I've gained.

I won.

POEMS

War paint drips down my cheeks
Clashes with my pale skin
My freckles: the infantry
Armed to the teeth
Guerrilla tactics fail
My war cry, a rebel yell
At odds with the enemy: myself

If my withered body
Could speak all the stifled words,
Tell of the aches and the pains,
The pleasures and the comforts,
Would you bother to listen?

Betrayal
Abandoned by the vessel
Rejected
Homeless inside four walls of flesh

Hope is a wild creature lurking in every corner
Whispering unknown languages
Capturing your attention
Creating a new being
Breathing life into an old carcass
Defining you
Opening you to a new realm of possibilities

I live in a sea of blankets
When I am more pain than person
Letting the Percocet flood my Corpus
As it numbs the neurons
Hoping it does its duty quickly or at all

Sleep eludes me
Panic drowns out the lethargy
Glazed eyes, heavy lids
An ache fills my bones
And yet anxiety demands an audience

Hope haunts me
Like a ghost from centuries past
Never like Casper, not gentle and kind
But a ghoul
Reminding me of something in my
periphery
Do I let the specter stay?

The skeleton inside me is begging to be free
To feel the dirt between its calcified toes
And the sea rush around its marrow core
Let the osteon flourish amidst the wildflowers

Bone cracking
Blood spilling
Muscle tearing
Sanity slipping
My body revolting:
To Overthrow the Dictator
Who has been in power too long.

The agony of it all
The broken-down body
The loneliness
Traces my outline like a seductive lover
Coaxing me to her
Breathing pain into my lungs,
Burning as I inhale
The misery of it all
Like a passionate tango
Dragging me across the dance floor,
An unwilling partner

It's tearing at my rationality.
My heart is pounding
like a racehorse at the final stretch
Chest heavy, head too light
Room spinning like I'm on a tilt-a-whirl
going way too fast.

The neurons of my body
Being twisted apart, slowly yet swiftly
Each one teasing me, agitating my soul
Hyperactive.
Energy flows through my bloodstream, erratically
Jumping off my insides
like an adult in a Bouncy Castle
Destroying it with each pulse

Crack. Snap. Splinter.
My body agonizes each sunrise
I greet it timidly
Hoping I don't awaken with fresh suffering

Drip.
The pain stammers in my ears.
Drip.
The fluid cold in my veins.
Drip.
The morphine shocks the system.
Drip.
Soothing weight, it coats the nerves.
Drip. Drip. Drop.
Coaxed into nothingness.

The IV hits a certain way
And the sweet violence of my heart beating
Rocks the cavities of my bones
Sweeps the blood cells through my veins
Swells my skin two sizes too big
And I'm a mess again

Such a sweet poison
Slipping into my veins
Dripping *"oh so quietly"*
Snaking its hypnotic venom
Deep inside me

I am in the middle of Love and Hate
With this body
I have been given.
She is here to help me
Yet denies me so much.
I fight the pain
And embrace the pleasure.
Hoping one day my body
Will be all that it should.

Pills sliding down my throat
Don't let me choke
Side effects sober me
Drug me
Take me down this Rabbit Hole

I miss my collarbones
I miss my dainty wrists
I miss my slender fingers
Now they are unrecognizable
All because of a pill
And its ravenous side effects

I want my old body back
Before the medication ravaged it
And distorted it
Gave it these after effects
And turned it into this wreckage

I am a prisoner to this bracelet fastened around my wrist.
Blood pressure cuffs and IVs ordained like jewelry
My energy and morale falter
Pharmaceuticals flow through my recovering blood vessels
The cheery nurse's bedside manner is anything but infectious
I can't wait to abandon this place.

Static breathing
Wistful thinking
Heartbeat racing
Morphine dripping
Fighting the heaviness
Entangled with my blood

A paradox of pain
Clinical, dialed in
Linoleum: too cold against bare feet
The air is stale and warm,
Letting the smells of vomit and medicine linger
This hospital room is all too familiar

Frustration seeping through my bones
Cracking the calcium at the core
Knocking me to my knees
My skeleton splinters.

A gully of anxiousness
Chest tightening like a tightrope line
Me - the acrobat walking over the Grand Canyon
The slackline disappearing with every inch forward
No net to catch me
Just a pit of black below

Sickeningly sweet stomach
Butterflies aflutter in my belly: Nerves.
You take a switchblade to them.
They swarm into yellow jackets.
Flaring up, stinging my throat and my gut.
Swelling me shut.

As I tear at the walls of my body, my home
I suffer and I bleed
The loathing bombards the scars, freckles, and stretch marks
I try to rebuild; to patch myself up with self-assurances
Building bricks of love and happiness
To not grow into any set mold
To blossom into a wildflower:
Fierce, delicate, blooming.

Burning. Snapping.
From my diaphragm
Trickling up
Scorching and tearing
Tightness- curling inward,
making it harder to breathe
Compression, like books crushing:
Bearing down on my ribs
Heartbeat in my ears
Not gushing, not rushing
A stagnant thump
Reminding me of my suffocation.

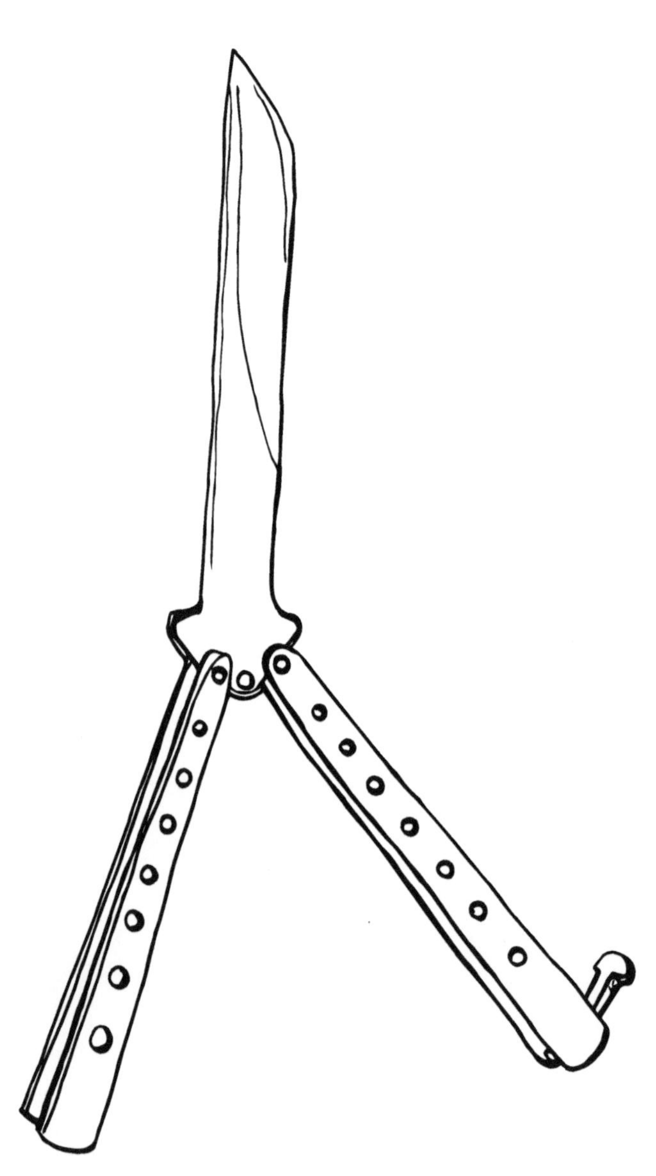

Pain is like robbery
It comes at night
In a dark alley
Cornering me at knifepoint
Stealing my sanity
My peace of mind
"This is a stick-up"
An assault on my senses

My body is my enemy
It is my sanctuary
I fight the agony, constant in its design
Adoring the ever-beating heart
Every breath is a reminder
I am at war
That I exist in two realities:
Pain and Pleasure

We sit here comparing wounds
"Mine is deeper"
Bleeding gaping flesh

It's almost 4 a.m.
Choking back the bile and the tears
...just have to make it to the next moment...
Breathe,

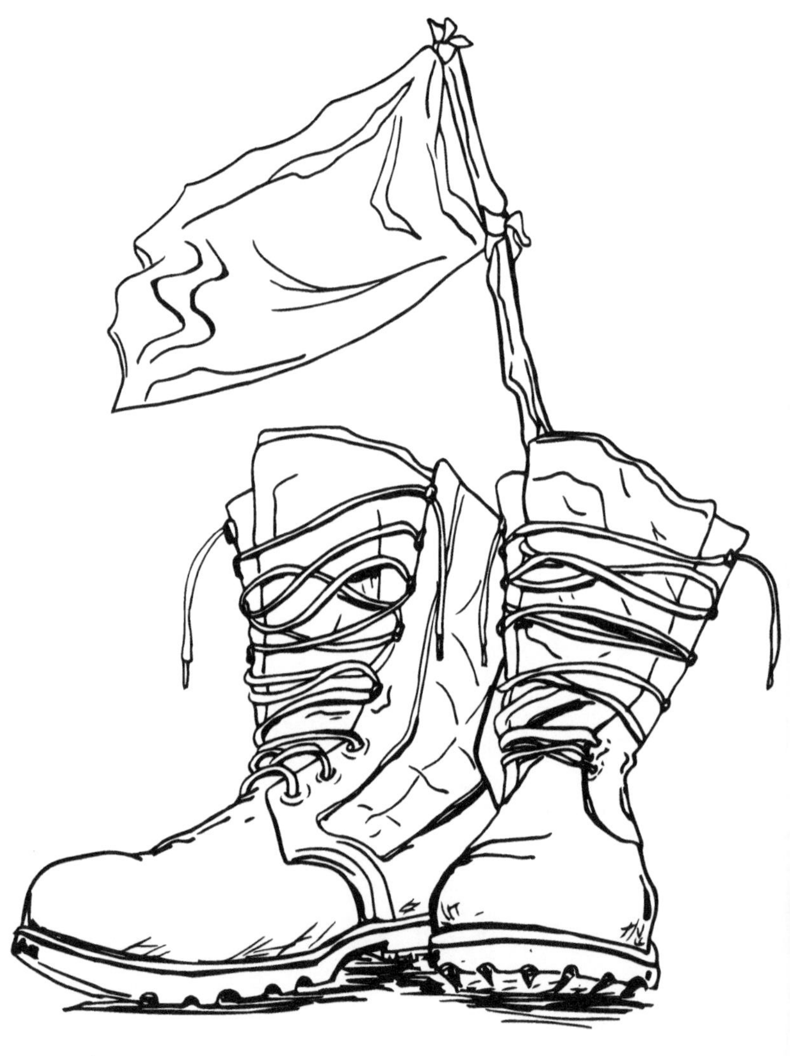

Waving my white flag
Surrendering to the Suffering
Too blinded by the bloodlust
Too preoccupied with engulfment of every nerve cell
Winning the battle over my fragmented body

I am humbled by my Pain
I am in awe of it
Could never fathom its evolution
How it ebbs and flows
Pulls me under
Then releases me
Just to drown me yet again
It's an ever-burning flame
Tickling my nerves
Yet can ignite a forest fire
Such an unpredictable enemy

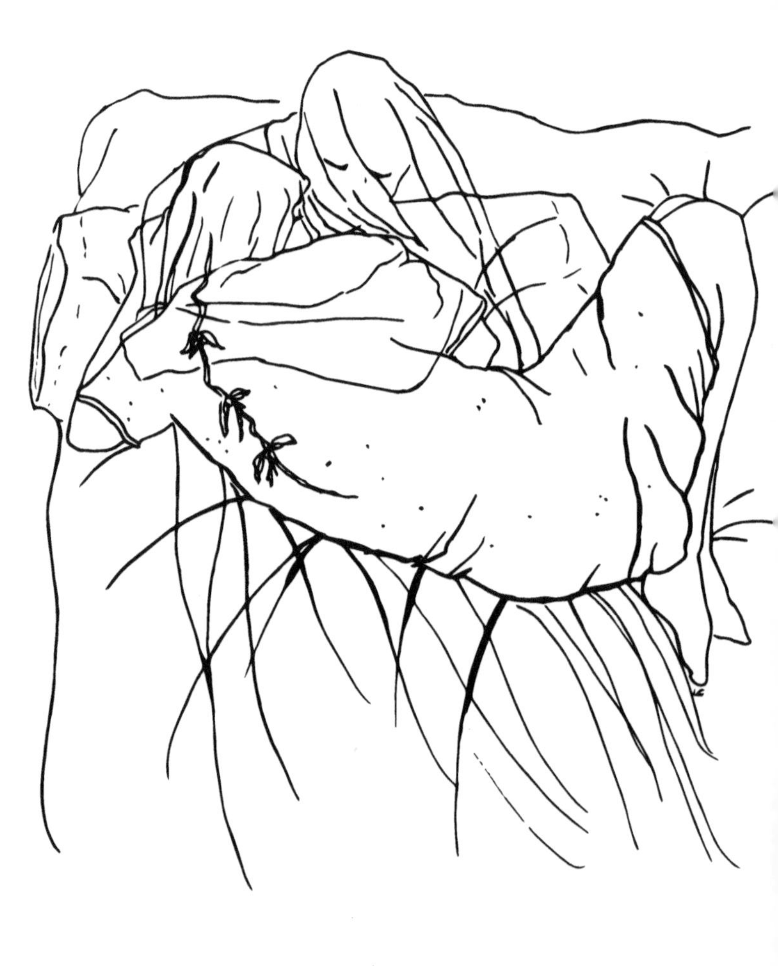

Hope, like a dim light in the morning
creeping into the bedroom,
crawling onto the sheets,
Illuminates with each passing second
Calm and slow, reaching for my body
to envelop my soul
To comfort me with its warmth.

Morphine

I feel myself slipping away, when a faint voice breaks through. A woman with kind eyes and latex gloves sits next to me; the process of quick relief has begun.

I hold my body still as I feel the medication slithering from the tube into my awaiting vein. In a second, my entire body tenses. The feeling of fire coursing through my blood vessels. I know the instant the pharmaceutical hits my brain.

I feel as if I am sinking down to the bottom of a swimming pool when the sun glints on the surface of the water and slightly blinds. I feel so heavy then.

Surrounded by a cocoon of numbness that seems to be suffocating me as each second passes. I cannot breathe. I still feel every pulsating beat of time.

I feel the blood throbbing into my head and every vein. The air cracking with anticipation like before a lightning strike, thick and humming.

My lungs begin to burn, and I quickly realize it had been too long since my last breath. A gray fog dances on the outside of my vision, but something inside me cannot breathe in.

I gasp as instincts take over. I inhale a crisp breath and feel a delicious numbing sensation encompass my body, melting my pain away like ice cream on a summer's day. I am warm, fuzzy, and content.

HOSPITAL HOSTAGE

I struggle to the doorframe that is only a few paces from my bed, peering out into the hallway with curiosity. Weakness engulfs my body; breathing becomes a task on its own. The whitewashed walls are pasted with light pastel paintings, dull in every aspect. A scale sits in the corner, off-kilter and unbalanced.

An elderly woman shuffles about while carrying a stack of manila folders. She chats animatedly with her coworker, as they gather papers. Both are dressed meticulously in white uniforms. A shriveled man sits in a wheelchair, cursing as he picks at his IV site. A mother hugs her young boy to her as she anxiously waits in a chair, surrounded by year-old magazines and a silent TV that is showing "All My Children".

I can faintly hear the beeps of a patient's heartbeat being monitored and the repeated rushing of an oxygen machine pumping air into someone's lungs. Hospital smells linger while masked by the potent smell of surface cleaner with a hint of pine, likely Pine-Sol.

As time drifts, the lights bleed into the walls and the background noise emphasizes the silence that hushes over the entire floor. I want to speak, to break the silence, but my voice is caught. My knees begin to wobble as I push my body to keep standing, fighting my exhausted state.

The tiling is cool against my bare feet and reminds me that I am a hostage to this band fastened around my wrist. The lack of stimulus provides no distractions and somehow the surroundings overload my senses. I can feel my body shutting down; nothing seems to make sense anymore. I lean against the door frame as my breathing becomes labored. Knots begin to form in my stomach and my vision blurs.

I slip now; my body won't allow me to continue to stand upright so I let myself fall. It doesn't hurt. I have become numb, an overload of pain assaulting every nerve cell in my body. I start to wretch as bile threatens my esophagus. I close my eyes; think about giving up. I am so tired and the blackness becomes a welcoming friend.

*Thank you for reading this. For giving my words your time.
This book was about giving my illness and disability its
acknowledgement, to show that I am stronger than the pain
I have gone through.
This book made it possible to stand on the other side.*

- Kelly

MY THOUGHTS AND LIFE
@WritesTheUnsaid on Instagram
KellyLynnCurry.com

Acknowledgments

To my mom, for always being my advocate and fighting for me when I could not do so for myself. Making sure I've gotten the best healthcare and showing me how I can be just as strong as you. For always having my best at heart.

To Matt, for reminding me I am stronger than I give myself credit for. For giving me the courage to stand up for myself and reminding me that I am "tough as nails". That I can make it from one second to the next because I have survived this long. You may say you do not understand poetry or creative writing, but you have inspired me so much in these words that I could not have done it without your support or inspiration.

To my brother, for always giving me your honest opinion, no matter what. You have always shown me what sheer determination looks like and what willpower can do. You remind me that you can do whatever you put your mind to and for fueling me with the best French macarons. Thank you.

To my dad, who always encourages my writing. You believe I can write the next best seller or the next best screenplay. For helping me find the right word or sentence. You never doubt my ability and it gives me the confidence to pursue my writing dreams.

I want to thank Laura Clift, for creating the etchings inside this book. You took my ideas and made them beautiful works of art. You took these poems and made beautiful works to coincide with them and I couldn't have asked for a better collaborator.

Finally, I want to thank Rachel Clift. Again. For collaborating on this book and making it what it is and bringing my words to life on the pages. I could never do what I've done without you. You help create dreams. You are so humble, and I am so lucky to have you help me make such beautiful work.

About the Author

Kelly Curry is a Spoonie based out of Lake Tahoe, California where she lives with a menagerie of animals. When not writing, Kelly collects books she plans to read. She believes that superheroes come in all shapes and sizes, kitten kisses cure most heartbreak, and sugar does help the medicine go down. This is her third collection of poetry.